real U®

## GUIDE TO

# ROAD SAFETY AND CAR CARE

## MEGAN STINE

## Real U Guides

**Publisher and CEO:**
Steve Schultz

**Editor-in-Chief:**
Megan Stine

**Art Director:**
C.C. Krohne

**Illustration:**
Mike Strong

**Production Manager:**
Alice Todd

**Editorial Assistant:**
Cody O. Stine

**Copy Editor:**
Leslie Fears

Library of Congress Control Number: 2004094760
ISBN: 1-932999-00-0

First Edition
10 9 8 7 6 5 4 3 2 1

Published by
Real U, Inc.
2582 Centerville Rosebud Rd.
Loganville, GA 30052

**www.realuguides.com**

Real U is a registered trademark of Real U, Inc.

# realU

## GUIDE TO

# ROAD SAFETY AND CAR CARE

## MEGAN STINE

# Throw Away This Book If...

Okay, we admit it. If you have a brand new car, half a brain, a credit card, a cell phone, an unlimited bank account, and membership in a roadside emergency service, you'll probably survive without reading this book.

But even if you have all that stuff, do you really want to spend all day some Saturday sitting by the side of the road in the pouring rain waiting for a tow-truck to arrive? Do you want to get your new $150 jeans all greasy changing a tire because your cell phone died or you wandered into a "no service" zone? And by the way, do you have any clue what the 10 best ways are to prevent a carjacking?

Yeah. There are some things money can't buy.

Which is why you may want to hang onto this book, even if your bank balance *is* bigger than the annual budget for a small developed nation.

Whether you're behind the wheel or under the hood, this guide has all the answers you need to stay safe in emergencies, avoid roadside disasters, and keep your car running smoothly without spending a fortune on mechanic's bills. (No promises on that last one, though. We haven't seen your car yet.)

So turn the page and check out all the great tips that are bound to make life on the road a lot easier.

And welcome to realU®

# GUIDE TO
# ROAD SAFETY AND CAR CARE
# TABLE OF CONTENTS

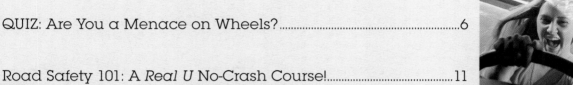

# ARE YOU A MENACE ON WHEELS?

**So you say you're as safe a driver as the next guy? That's great! Unless, of course, the next guy happens to be that neighbor of yours whose car looks like it's been through one too many massive rock slides and who treats parallel parking like it's some kind of demolition derby.**

Even if you are a better driver than the average Steve McQueen stand-in, you could still be a menace to yourself and others if you don't take care of your car—if, for example, the last time you changed your wiper blades was during the Carter administration. Before you take your life in your hands again, try taking this quiz to find out if you and your car are likely to survive longer than, well, the Carter administration.

# You could still be a menace to yourself and others if you don't take care of your car.

## 1.

Let's say you're cruising down the highway and you're having a hard time reading the extensive collection of bumper stickers on the car in front of you. This is because...

**A.** That joker in front of you keeps speeding up in spite of your efforts to stay right on his tail at all costs.

**B.** You're maintaining a safe following distance by using the 3-second rule.

**C.** You "forgot" to wear your glasses, which are required for driving, but which your friends say make you look like an IRS auditor.

## 2.

So when did you change your wiper blades, anyway?

**A.** Wiper blades...you're supposed to change them?

**B.** Let's see, what time is it? 4:00? So, like, maybe three hours ago. Four hours tops.

**C.** Hard to say—most of Europe was still on the Julian calendar, so the calculation is a bit tricky.

*your windshield?*

# What's the left lane for?

## 3.

Imagine you're driving on the highway in rush hour traffic, your cell phone is ringing, and you've got an extra value meal in a bag on the seat next to you. As you're merging into the far left lane, what do you reach for first?

**A.** The fries.

**B.** Your turn signal.

**C.** A ketchup packet for the fries. Or maybe the burger, then the ketchup, then the fries.

## 4.

**Speaking of the far left lane, what's it for?**

**A.** Getting to the mall in a hurry so you can beat the crowds.

**B.** Passing slower moving traffic, when necessary.

**C.** Only the strong and bold of spirit—and everyone else had better stay the heck out of your way.

*not a good idea!*

Where's the blind spot?

## 5.

**Most truckers have a blind spot...**

**A.** But you pass them so fast, it doesn't really matter.

**B.** Along both sides of their trailer, 10 or 20 feet in front of the cab, and about 200 feet behind the trailer.

**C.** Where their fashion sense should be.

# SCORING

**First of all, if you read this quiz while driving, you're immediately disqualified, and should give us your keys until you've read this book from cover to cover. However...**

### If you answered mostly A's:

We're not saying we'd never ride in your car...but we might start bringing protective headgear if you don't get your act together soon.

### If you answered mostly B's:

Great! You've obviously got your head in the right place about driving— and probably your jumper cables and tire gauge in their right places, too. However, even you could probably use a refresher course about keeping your car—and your driving record—in good shape. So read on.

### If you answered mostly C's:

O.K., pull over to the side of the road, chief. Now, do you have any idea why we stopped you? No? And that, my friend, is why you need this book.

You alone can make the difference between whether you come through most driving emergencies with nothing more than a headache, or wind up with a major concussion.

# ROAD SAFETY 101: A REAL U NO-CRASH COURSE

**Relax. We aren't going to spew a lot of grizzly statistics at you about how many drivers are killed on the road each year. We've saved that stuff for Page 21.**

But there's one statistic you need to keep in mind when you get behind the wheel of a car: The majority of all people killed in traffic crashes (a whopping 65%, in fact) are drivers.

Bottom line is you're in charge, and you alone can make the difference between whether you come through most driving emergencies with nothing more than a headache, or wind up with a major concussion.

So turn the page and read on to learn all the basics that could save your life, including what to pack in your roadside emergency kit, how to drive safely in bad weather, and the 10 best ways to avoid crashes.

Oh, and for the 10 best ways to avoid reading grizzly statistics? Don't turn to Page 21.

*no cell phone...*

# JUNK FOR YOUR TRUNK:

## WHAT TO PACK IN A ROADSIDE EMERGENCY SURVIVAL KIT

### GOTTA HAVES

- Cell phone
- Spare tire, properly inflated
- Jack
- Crossbar lug wrench
- Flashlight and extra batteries
- Jumper cables
- Bottled water
- First aid kit

Admit it. Your idea of a roadside emergency kit is 4 great CD's including something mellow, something acoustic, and some oldies; a box of breath mints; a pair of spare pantyhose; and the phone numbers of 3 friends with enough gossip and/or sports scores to keep you entertained while you wait for AAA to arrive.

That works—as long as your cell phone doesn't die and you don't get a flat tire in a low cell phone service area.

But in case you're not so lucky, here's a list of the stuff you ought to keep in your trunk for emergencies.

### DON'T LEAVE HOME WITHOUT...

This stuff doesn't go in the trunk, but you should always have with you in your car: your driver's license, registration, and proof of insurance. In some states, you're required by law to carry a copy of the insurance policy, too, not just the insurance cards.

cell phones are a must-have in an emergency!

## SHOULD HAVES

- Work gloves
- Rags and hand cleaner
- Flares, or emergency warning triangles, or highway safety sticks
- Blanket
- Empty gas can
- Length of hollow pipe (for adding leverage to your tire iron)
- WD-40 (great for getting lug nuts off)
- Energy snack bars
- Cardboard "CALL POLICE" sign
- Disposable camera (to record damage after a collision)
- Pen and notebook (for taking notes after a collision)
- Emergency money (Keep $20 in an envelope in the glove compartment and don't kid yourself—"out of beer" is not an emergency.)

## FOR OLDER CARS

- Tool kit including screwdriver and pliers
- Duct tape (handy for emergency repairs of leaky hoses)

## IN WINTER CLIMATES

- Ice scraper
- Small snow shovel
- Cat litter or bag of sand (for traction)
- Extra blankets

glad I bought that scraper!

# 10 BEST WAYS TO AVOID CRASHES

## 1.

### ADJUST YOUR MIRRORS CORRECTLY

Forget what you were taught about how your side-view mirrors should be adjusted. Turns out, it's wrong. Experts now say that there's no point in being able to see the back corner of your car in your mirror because—guess what?—it isn't going anywhere and it's not likely to smash into you. (Who knew?) Instead, angle your mirrors out a bit, as shown on Page 16, to reduce or even eliminate your blind spot. (Sorry, there's nothing we can do about your bald spot.)

## 2.

### USE A 3-SECOND GAP BY DAY, A 6-SECOND GAP BY NIGHT

We're not talking about the length of time between cell phone calls here, either. We're talking about the trick that helps you know whether you're following too close to the car in front of you. Here's how it works: Pick out a stationary object or landmark in the distance—a tree, house, or 60-foot giant sculptural peach painted on a water tower. Whatever. Start counting when the car in front of you passes it. One thousand one, one thousand two, one thousand three... You shouldn't pass that same object yourself in less than 3 seconds in the daytime. If you do, you're following too close to the car in front of you and may not be able to stop in time in an emergency. At night or in bad weather, double the time to 6 seconds. The 3-second gap is a better rule of thumb than the older method of using one car length for every 10 mph you're traveling. Problems arise, however, when you use a moving object as the landmark, such as a galloping horse, speeding locomotive, or Superman.

*are you far enough away if that car stops suddenly?*

# 3.

## HANG UP AND DRIVE

More than 1.5 million people were involved in crashes that involved cell phone use in the past 5 years. It's against the law to talk on a cell phone while driving in many states—unless you're using a hands-free device. And if the statistics are any proof, it should be illegal everywhere. If you've got to make or take a cell phone call, get off the roadway completely. (Only exception: if you're calling a funeral home to arrange your own funeral.) See the box below for more about how cell phone use, and other distractions, can affect your driving.

# 4.

## WATCH OUT AT INTERSECTIONS

Maybe you think you won't become one of the 8,000 people who die in an intersection crash in a typical year. But do you really want to be one of the 2.7 million who survive intersection crashes? Nearly 1/3 of these people sustain injuries and the other 2/3 don't like the looks of their vehicles afterward. Best plan: Don't become part of the intersection crash statistics at all. Slow down whenever you approach an intersection, especially a busy one, stay extra alert, and assume that someone is going to run that red light or barrel through that stop sign.

According to the National Highway Traffic Safety Administration, distractions are a factor in 50% of all collisions. Distractions can be physical—a stranger waving at you, for instance. Or they can be intellectual—having a heated conversation with your best friend. Distractions can come from inside or outside the vehicle. Talking on a cell phone while driving is only one of the distractions that can be very dangerous. Other common distractions include operating A/V equipment, talking to passengers, eating, drinking, and daydreaming.

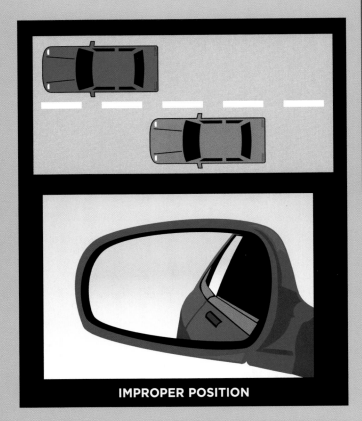

**IMPROPER POSITION**

**PROPER POSITION**

On the road, you should be able to see a car in your rearview when it's behind you, and then immediately in your left side-view mirror as it passes.

# HOW TO ADJUST YOUR OUTSIDE MIRRORS

1. **Adjust your rearview mirror as you normally would.**

2. **Lean your head to the left and rest it against the driver's side window.**

   With your head against the glass, adjust your left side mirror as you normally would— so you can see just a bit of the left side of your car.

3. **Lean to the right about the same amount as you leaned to the left.**

   Adjust your right side mirror the same way.

4. **Return to a normal driving position and test your mirrors out.**

   You won't be able to see the side of your own car now, but that's okay. You'll be seeing more of what used to be a blind spot. On the road, you should be able to see a car in your rearview when it's behind you, and then immediately in your left side-view mirror as it passes. Blind spot— gone!

> **Don't drive with more than one friend in the car until you've been driving for at least a year.**

*passengers are distracting*

# 5.
## LEAVE YOURSELF AN OUT

This is a simple rule: Don't move your car into a position on the road where you can't possibly escape if something unexpected happens. For instance, if you're passing a truck on the right, on the highway, and there's only a guardrail with a 50-ft. drop to your right, what are you going to do if the truck suddenly decides to move into your lane? This isn't such an unlikely scenario, by the way, since trucks have very long blind spots along both sides. Look ahead at the landscape, barriers, and traffic patterns, and don't put your car between a rock and a hard place.

# 6.
## GO ONE ON ONE

Best thing about having a car when you're young? Being able to haul a load of your friends around on a Saturday night. Unfortunately, that's also the best way to wreck your car if you're a new driver. Best friends can be pretty distracting, especially when they're all talking at once and you're trying to hold up your end of the conversation. Best idea: Don't drive with more than one friend in the car until you've been driving for at least a year. (Some states even have laws prohibiting you from taking passengers until you're an experienced driver.) Experienced drivers shouldn't underestimate how distracting passengers can be, either. See tip #7 for the ugly truth about soccer moms.

# 7.
## LET THE KIDS SCREAM

When it comes to distractions that lead to collisions, screaming kids in the backseat account for nearly one-fifth of all the trouble—and soccer moms and dads are the culprits. In fact, screaming, crying, fussing, fighting, squabbling, whining and cranky kids are among the top 4 causes of crashes. So ask yourself: Do I really need to turn around and settle that fight now? It's better to ignore the kids until you've reached your destination, or pull over and deal with it while the car is stopped. Take our word for it—in most cases, they can't hurt themselves or each other anywhere near as much as you can hurt them if you wreck the car.

You'd be surprised by how many people wreck their cars each year because they were looking for an address.

# 8.

## DON'T OVERCORRECT OR OVERREACT

Let's say there's one of those oversized, too-much-testosterone SUV's coming toward you in the opposite lane, and you can tell he's over the yellow line, swerving onto your side of the road. Your impulse is to yank your car to the right to get out of the way, right? Whoops—now you're off the road on the shoulder. So you jerk the wheel to the left and...uh-oh. Ouch. That SUV was even bigger and heavier than you thought. Over-steering in an emergency is a common mistake made by inexperienced drivers, especially on the highway. Try to remember that the faster you're going, the more quickly your car will respond to steering changes. Try to react to emergencies by staying calm and looking where you want the car to go, *not* at what you want to miss. Steer just the right amount to put your car where it needs to be.

Alcohol, other drugs, fatigue, sleepiness and emotions all cause driver impairments. Don't drive unless you are physically and mentally fit.

# 9.

## PULL OVER IF YOU'RE LOST

You'd be surprised by how many people wreck their cars each year because they were looking for an address or a street sign, or missed the turn for the all-night carry-out where they were going to pick up a six-pack of beer. Moral of the story: If you're lost, pull over and check a map or phone for directions while the car is stopped. If you think you missed the exit for your grandmother's 90th birthday party, pull over and formulate a plan. If the plan involves heading straight back to the all-night carry out, read on and memorize #10 below.

# 10.

## DON'T DRINK AND DRIVE

It's so obvious, we put it last. But it's so important, we couldn't leave it off the list. Designate a non-drinking driver, or call a cab, or sleep on the host's bathroom floor, or phone a grumpy neighbor and beg him to come pick you up. Whatever. Just don't get behind the wheel. And if you're the designated driver for friends after a late-night party, be extra careful. The greatest number of fatal traffic crashes happen between the hours of midnight and 3:00 a.m. on Saturday night—just about the time when you might be heading home.

# STORMY WEATHER

## RULES FOR DRIVING IN RAIN, SLEET, SNOW, AND ICE

- Use your headlights any time you use your windshield wipers.

- Slow down in rain and sleet, but don't go too slow in deep snow. You may need momentum to keep the car moving forward in deep snow.

- Remember that the road is slipperier when it first starts raining, as rain mixes with the build-up of oil and grease on the road surface.

- Apply brakes more gently on wet and icy surfaces.

- Keep headlights on low beam in fog and rain.

- Pull off the road if you can't see the side of the road or the center line.

- Use your A/C, even in cold weather, to defog your windshield. The A/C will work, even on a warm or "heater" setting, to remove moisture from the air.

Pull off the road if you can't see the center line.

# HOW TO RECOVER FROM A SKID

1. **Take your foot off the gas gradually and don't touch the brake!**

2. **Look in the direction you want to go and calmly steer that way.**

3. **Try to avoid the impulse to hit the brake.**
   That's more likely to make you slip and slide even more.

4. **Don't panic and don't overcorrect.**
   Just keeping looking toward the direction you want to go and steer toward your goal.

*too rainy for cruise control*

## CRUISE CONTROL CAUTIONS

Don't use cruise control on any surface with reduced traction such as wet, snowy, icy, sandy, or gravelly roads. Doing so can lead to a loss of traction, followed by a skid and a collision. It's also a bad idea to use cruise control in heavy traffic, or on hilly or mountainous terrain. Check your owner's manual for more tips about how and when it should be used.

# GRIZZLY STATISTICS

| GRIZZLY STATISTICS | WHAT YOU SHOULD DO ABOUT IT |
|---|---|
| 1 out of 3 drivers use cell phones while driving. | Be very afraid of about 1/3 of all the cars on the road. |
| 75% of all passengers who were completely ejected from a car died. | Wear your seatbelt. Duh. |
| Night driving is 3 times as dangerous as daylight driving. | Slow down, stay extra alert, and leave more space between you and the car in front of you at night. |
| Front seat occupants are 5 times as likely to die in a car crash if the back seat occupants aren't buckled up. | Make your back seat passengers wear their seat belts—for your own sake as well as theirs! |
| You are 5 times as likely to die in a rollover crash than in a non-rollover collision. | Choose a car that is less likely to roll over. Also, slow down on curves, where the most common types of rollover crashes happen. |
| Auto crashes are the leading cause of death for 15- to 20-year-olds. | Assume you're at a greater than average risk if you ride with someone in this age group. |
| 29% of teen drivers who were killed in car crashes had been drinking. | Don't make us say it again: DON'T DRINK AND DRIVE. |

help!

# WHEN DISASTER STRIKES: HOW TO HANDLE DRIVING EMERGENCIES

**Some roadside "emergencies" are pretty lame. Running out of gas, for instance, or locking your keys in the car aren't going to ruin your life.**

Those are just two examples of things you'll kick yourself for, and so what? Kicking yourself isn't likely to result in death or even bodily injury (unless you're a contortionist).

Other kinds of emergencies, however, are more dire, and you may wind up being a bit rattled if something really scary happens— if your tire blows out when you're pushing 70 mph on a highway full of truckers, for example.

That's why it's a good idea to scope out the worst case scenarios ahead of time. So read this chapter, even if you don't read anything else in this book. Why? Because if you plunge off a bridge into an icy river in your car, we can guarantee you won't have time to fish this book out of the glove compartment to find out what to do.

# EMERGENCY 101
# STRANDED!

## WHAT TO DO IF YOUR CAR BREAKS DOWN ON THE ROAD

Whether it's a tire blowout, an over-heated radiator, an empty gas tank, or you simply ate too many tacos at your cousin's bachelor blast...in an emergency, you'll want to get off the road as safely and quickly as possible. Follow these basic steps.

1. **Hit the flashers and check your mirrors.**
   Then pull to the side of the road. Get as far off the road as you can.

2. **Get out of the car carefully.**
   Use the passenger side door to avoid opening a door into traffic.

3. **Decide whether this is a problem you can handle yourself.**
   You may be able to change a flat tire, for instance—especially if you have this guide in the car. See Page 27 for tips. If you can't handle the repair yourself, go on to step 4.

4. **Raise the hood as a signal that you need help.**

5. **Get back in the car and lock the doors.**
   Sit on the passenger side, farthest away from traffic.

6. **If you have a cell phone, use it to call a family member or friend.**
   Explain that you're stranded and be prepared to give them your location. Then call AAA or whatever other emergency roadside service you have a membership in.

7. **If you don't have a cell phone, put a sign in the rear window that says, "Emergency—Call Police."**

8. **If someone stops and offers to help, don't get out of the car.**
   Crack the window an inch and ask them to call the police. Tell them you'd rather wait in the car for the police to arrive.

9. **Wait for help to arrive.**

10. **In some situations, you may decide to walk to get help.**
    If so, leave a note on your dashboard with your name, the date and time when you left the car, and the direction you're walking. Leave your hood open, but do not leave your flashers going—this can drain your battery completely, causing more problems. Remember that it's never a good idea to accept rides with strangers.

*Think you can fix it yourself? Turn the page for tips*

**Remember that it's never a good idea to accept rides with strangers.**

# BLOWOUT!

A flat tire in your driveway is an annoyance, but it's not the kind of thing you need a laminated, illustrated, 40-page escape plan to handle. A flat tire while you're cruising down the highway is a different matter—and while it may not take 40 pages of do's and don't's to deal with it, you will want to keep a few tips in mind.

Here's what you'll need to know if you blow a tire while you're on the road:

**1 Do not slam on the brakes.**
It's difficult to control a car with a flat tire, and braking will only make it more difficult.

**2 Slow down by taking your foot off the gas.**
Keep both hands on the wheel to steady the car.

**3 Turn on your flashers to let others know you are having trouble.**

**4 Only after you've slowed down to less than 30 mph should you start braking.**
When you do brake, do it gingerly at first, and be prepared for the car to be difficult to handle. Keep both hands on the wheel.

**5 Get over to the side of the road as soon as you safely can.**
The key word here is "safely"— don't panic, and don't swerve in front of traffic. Merge as you normally would.

**6 Don't worry if you have to drive a few extra feet in order to get off the road safely.**
You should not, however, drive all the way to the nearest service station, or to your best friend's or parents' house, unless it happens to be right across the street. You can do serious damage to your car if you drive on a flat tire for very long. You might also lose control of the car.

**7 Changing a tire on the side of the highway can be difficult and dangerous.**
Even if you've changed a tire before, it's best to call a roadside emergency service for help if you have a blow-out on a busy or otherwise treacherous stretch of road.

**8 Whether you change the tire yourself or wait for a pro to come help, you'll probably need some of the things in your emergency kit.**
What emergency kit? See Page 12.

# HOW TO CHANGE A TIRE

**First off, let's be completely honest: Changing a tire is probably the least fun you can have with a lug wrench.**

But the only really difficult thing about changing a tire is loosening the lugs—the nuts or bolts (depending on your car) which hold the tire on the wheel. Why? Because the last time your lug nuts were tightened, it was probably by a mechanic, who probably used an air wrench, which probably got them so tight it would take half the Prussian army to get them off. So here's one of the most important tire-changing tips we can offer: Don't let the mechanic tighten your lug nuts with an air wrench! Ask him to tighten them by hand. Then you'll be able to loosen them yourself, by hand, when the time comes.

Whether or not changing your tire is going to be an epic battle between man and machine, the basic requirements will be the same.

**1. The first step is to make sure you've got enough room to maneuver on the necessary side of the car.**
If you're contemplating changing a tire on the side of a busy highway or road, contemplate again, unless you've got a lot of clearance between where you'll be bending over and where cars will be whizzing past. Call for professional help if you don't feel comfortable.

**2. Put the car in park, or in first gear if it's a manual. Put the emergency brake on.**
If there are passengers in the car, have them get out and move to a safe location. Get psyched. Don't jack up the car yet—that step comes later.

### 3. Once you're psyched and raring to go, the first step is the rather demoralizing one of trying to loosen the lug nuts.

A crossbar style lug wrench can be very helpful. So can a can of WD-40, and a four-foot length of metal or very strong PVC pipe, slightly wider than the handle of your lug wrench, which you can slip over the lug wrench for better leverage. You may be tempted to stand on the end of your lug wrench—and in fact, you may be convinced this is the only way you'll ever make any progress—but be warned: You can actually break your lug nuts by standing on the wrench. This not only ruins your chances of changing the tire, but it can be expensive to fix, too. Jump up and down on the wrench at your own risk.

### 4. Once you get the lug nuts loose, do not take them all the way off.

Loosen them until they're a couple turns from off.

### 5. The next step is to jack up the car, with the flat tire still hanging on.

You can't put the jack just anywhere, though. Check your owner's manual to find out where your "jack points" are— the places on the car body where it's safe to put the jack. There should be at least four of these—one by each tire—and if you don't put the jack under one of the jack points, you risk damaging the body of the car, or even worse, having the car fall off the jack. Raise the car until the flat tire is several inches off the ground. Remember that you'll need more clearance for a full-sized spare—which isn't flat—than for the currently flat tire.

### 6. Now loosen the lugs the rest of the way.

As you take the nuts (or bolts) off, put them on the ground in the position they were in on the car. That way you can put them back in the same spots they came from. If you're smart, you'll leave the top lug for last—otherwise the tire starts to tip, and it's harder to get the other lug nuts off.

## 7. Take the tire off. It's easiest to remove if you grab it at the 9:00 and 3:00 positions.

Hang the spare tire on the studs. (If you have a European car with lug bolts, there are no studs on which to hang the wheel. You'll have to line it up with the holes and then put one of the bolts—preferably the top one—back in with your other hand.) Wipe the sweat from your brow.

## 8. Put the lugs back on.

Tighten them in a criss-cross pattern, starting with the one at the top (or twelve o'clock) position. Tighten them by hand at first, and then tighten each of them about one more turn with the lug wrench.

## 9. Lower the jack, and then tighten the lugs nice and tight with the lug wrench.

What's nice and tight? Your manual should list a "torque requirement," but the only way to measure this is with a torque wrench, which you probably don't have. The best bet is to lean against the lug wrench with most of your weight, but not to jump up and down on it. Remember to use the criss-cross pattern. (See the illustration.) Lug nuts that are tightened in the wrong sequence can damage your brake discs or drums.

Remember, if you've got a "doughnut spare"—an undersized spare tire—you can't drive on it for very long, and some doughnuts have a speed limit as well. You'll have to get it replaced right away.

# TIGHTENING LUG NUTS

**Tighten the bolts in a criss-cross pattern, starting with the bolt at the top.**

**4 LUG NUTS**

**5 LUG NUTS**

# WHAT TO DO WHEN YOU RUN OUT OF GAS

**Stop. Pull over.**
**Like you have any choice.**
**What are you going to do?**
**Coast?**

Running out of gas is one of those emergencies that doesn't leave you with many options. The one thing to remember is that you do get a few seconds of warning before the car totally dies, and you should use those seconds to get your car off the road and out of traffic. You'll know those few seconds have arrived when you've been running on empty and all of a sudden you either feel the car lose its momentum—as if the engine is about to stall—or hear a sputtering, coughing sound which isn't coming from your asthmatic cousin Rupert. That's the sound of your engine not having enough gas to run; it'll usually only last about five seconds before you hear, see, and feel the sound of your engine not running at all, so act fast. Pull as far off the road as possible, and then call for help.

Or better yet, buy a tank of gas, you lousy cheapskate.

## REMEMBER
**You get a few seconds of warning before the car totally dies. You should use those seconds to get your car off the road and out of traffic.**

# So you missed the gas station and you're running low.
## WHAT DO YOU DO?

1. **Consider turning around.**
   Going back 2 miles may be better than walking 10 or 20 miles to get help.

2. **Turn off the air conditioner.**
   Air conditioners use extra gasoline.

3. **Shut the windows.**
   Open windows cause drag.

4. **Slow your speed down.**
   Slower speeds use less gas.

5. **Coast down hills.**
   This saves the most gas.

6. **Go ahead and move to the right lane.**
   Then you'll be ready if you run out of gas.

7. **Turn your flashers on.**
   This will alert other drivers that you're traveling very slowly because you know you're about out of gas.

*I made it to the gas station!*

# JOIN THE CLUB?

Everyone's heard of AAA—they're the biggest and most well-known auto club in America. But do you always have to hang with the popular crowd? Not necessarily. There are other ways to get many of the same roadside emergency services for less than the current average $55 cost of AAA membership. (Membership fees vary from state to state.) Many auto insurance companies offer emergency road service coverage as an option on your policy, some for as little as $12 a year. All provide about the same services when your battery is dead, your tire is flat, or your gas tank is empty. (None are very helpful when you leave your windows down in the car wash, forget to make your car payment on time, or are simply having a bad hair day.) AAA offers an array of other goodies, however, that you don't get from most insurance companies: free maps, free travel guide books, free traveler's checks, and more. Whichever you choose, it's probably a good idea to have some kind of road service, if only for the peace of mind.

# HOW TO JUMP-START A CAR

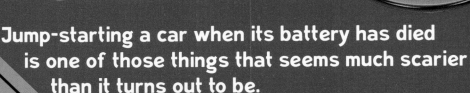

**Jump-starting a car when its battery has died is one of those things that seems much scarier than it turns out to be.**

But there's a good reason to be moderately afraid: If you do it wrong, you can create a massive hydrogen explosion that can result in injury or death. Many people are injured each year in the process. Follow these instructions carefully and precisely, and you shouldn't have any problems. If you are hesitant or unsure, call for road service and let a professional handle it.

## CAUTIONS!

■ **DO NOT connect the positive terminal to the negative terminal of either battery!**
It will cause an explosion. Connect only positive to positive.

■ **DO NOT connect the negative terminals of the two batteries!**
The negative terminal of the dead battery is not used in a jump-start. Connecting it can cause an explosion when sparks ignite hydrogen gas fumes from the battery.

■ **DO NOT touch the positive connector of the jumper cables to the car body!**
The car body is actually connected to the negative terminal on the battery, so that can cause an explosion.

■ **NEVER assume there is no charge in a "dead" battery.**
It may not be enough to start your car, but it may be enough to cause serious bodily harm.

■ **NEVER touch the battery terminals with your hands!**
Also, once you've begun this procedure, never touch the metal clamp on the jumper cables with your hands.

■ **DO NOT let the ends of the jumper cables touch each other once you've started.**
Make sure to keep them separated.

■ **DO NOT let the ends of the jumper cables touch a source of water.**

# 1.

## Park the cars nose to nose and turn off both engines.

Take the keys out of the ignitions, just to be extra-careful. You'll need to put the two cars—the dead one and the one that's still kicking—close enough for your jumper cables to reach from one engine to the other, but make sure the cars aren't touching in any way.

*make sure the cars aren't touching*

# 2.

## Attach a red-handled positive clamp to the positive terminal on the dead battery.

This assumes that your jumper cables are red and black, as most jumper cables are. (If yours are red and yellow, no problem. Just pretend the yellow one is black and read on.) The positive terminal will look like a big bolt, and should be marked with a plus sign (+). Don't touch the metal part of the clamp at any time!

# 3.

## Attach the other red-handled clamp to the positive terminal on the live battery.

Remember how you weren't supposed to touch the metal part of the clamp in Step 2? Well, you're still not.

# 4.

## Attach the black-handled negative clamp to the negative terminal on the live battery.

Caution! Once you've done this, the jumper cables have electricity running through them, and so you really can't touch the metal parts of the clamps, or the terminals of the batteries, or anything else. Turn the page for Step 5.

- **MAKE SURE the jumper cables will not interfere with any moving parts, once the dead engine is started.**

- **DO NOT attempt to jump-start antique foreign cars, as the ground terminals may be different.**

typical battery →

## 5.
### Attach the other black-handled clamp to a piece of metal inside the dead car's engine.

Do NOT attach it to the negative terminal of the battery. Instead, find an exposed bolt or clamp somewhere in the engine, and attach the clamp to it.

If you haven't yet blown anything up, you're not going to. Congratulations!

## 6.
### Start the live car.

Let it run for two or three minutes. Rev the engine a little bit for good measure.

# CONNECTING THE JUMPER CABLES

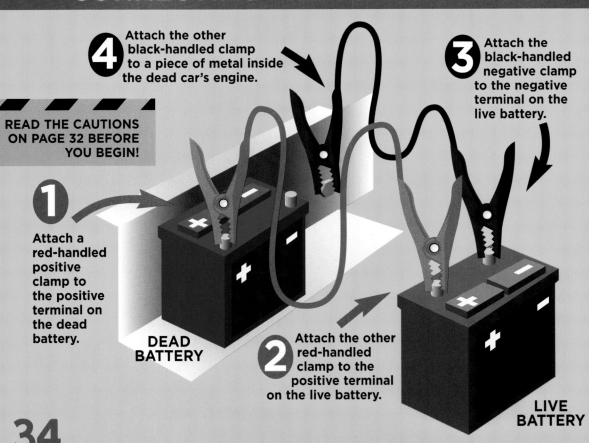

**4** Attach the other black-handled clamp to a piece of metal inside the dead car's engine.

**3** Attach the black-handled negative clamp to the negative terminal on the live battery.

**READ THE CAUTIONS ON PAGE 32 BEFORE YOU BEGIN!**

**1** Attach a red-handled positive clamp to the positive terminal on the dead battery.

DEAD BATTERY

**2** Attach the other red-handled clamp to the positive terminal on the live battery.

LIVE BATTERY

*my battery's dead!!*

## 7.

### Try to start the dead car.

If it doesn't start after a few tries, there may be rust on the clamps or on the battery terminals. Shut off both cars and reconnect the cables, making sure that the jumper clamps really dig into the battery terminals (cutting through any rust). If this doesn't work after three or four tries, you should not keep trying—if you can't jump-start the car, it may have electrical problems, which could be made worse by continued attempts. Get it to a mechanic and have it looked at.

## 8.

### Let it idle before carefully disconnecting.

Once the dead car has idled for a while, with the car still on, disconnect the jumper cables in the reverse order that you attached them. (For those of you who can't read backward, disconnect them in this order: 1. Negative cable on the dead car. 2. Negative cable on the live car. 3. Positive cable on the live car. 4. Positive cable on the dead car.) Don't touch the clamps! And don't let the clamps touch each other, either! No touching!

## 9.

### Let it run.

Don't shut off the recently-dead car for a while; let it run for a few more minutes. Then drive it around for twenty minutes to let the battery recharge.

Jump-starting may not be a permanent fix if you've got a bad battery—if you've had to jump-start your car several times for no good reason (i.e., you didn't leave the lights on, but the battery died anyway), you may have a bad battery.

Of course, these simple steps don't work nearly as well if you don't happen to own jumper cables, and have to use your imagination. So make sure to keep a set of jumper cables in your car, preferably with a copy of this book, so you know how to use them. (For more on what you should keep in your car at all times, see Page 12.)

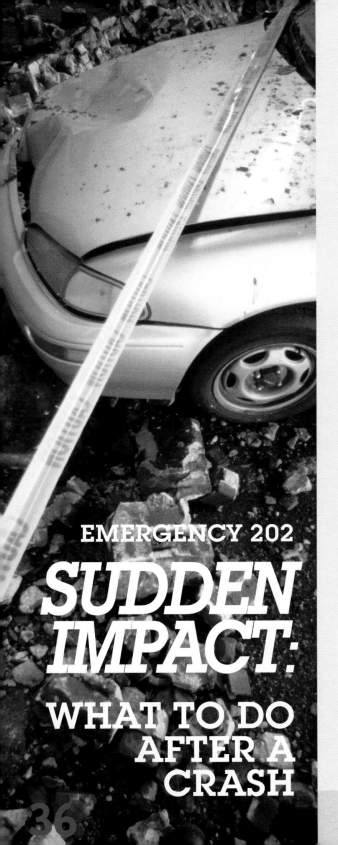

# SUDDEN IMPACT:

## WHAT TO DO AFTER A CRASH

**Unlike the buzz you used to get from ramming your bumper car into your dad's when you were a kid, auto crashes aren't much fun.**

So we're skipping the jokes and going straight to the hardcore advice. Memorize this page, and then toss the book in your glove compartment—you'll probably be too freaked out if you do have a crash to remember half this stuff.

### 1. Check for injuries.

Stay calm and deal with health and safety issues first. Do not move an injured person unless there is an immediate danger or a possibility of even greater injury. Moving an injured person can aggravate the injuries. Call 911 and let the pros handle the situation. If possible, cover the injured person with a blanket to keep the person warm. Also, don't offer water to someone who's been injured—it can make the situation worse if he or she chokes.

### 2. Set up flares or other warning devices in the road to alert oncoming traffic.

Also turn on your flashers.

### 3. Call the police, even if the collision is minor.

If someone was injured or the crash was serious, don't move your car. Stay at the scene until the police arrive, complete their investigation, and say you may leave. Get the officer's name and the police report incident number, and ask how to get a copy of the report.

### 4. Don't admit fault.

You may not be aware of all the circumstances that led to the collision. The other driver may be more at fault than you realize. Don't discuss the collision with anyone except the police and your insurance company. When you speak to the police, tell the truth but don't try to determine who is to blame.

## 5. Exchange information.

Write down the names, addresses, phone numbers, license plate numbers, insurance company and policy numbers, and driver's license numbers for every person involved in the crash. You should also get the VIN number for the other car or cars—the license plate isn't enough. Note the make, model, color, and description of the other car. If there were passengers in the other car, be sure to get their info as well. Find out whether the insurance is in the driver's name. If not, get the name of the insured.

## 6. Photograph the crash scene.

Use the disposable camera you bought right after you read Page 13—the camera that is now in the glove compartment of your car—to document the damage to all vehicles involved. In addition to close-ups, take some pictures that show the overall scene and setting where the crash happened. And be sure to shoot the undamaged sides of each car as well as the damaged. This comes in handy if the other driver manages to wreck his car again, a few days later, and tries to blame the subsequent damage on you.

## 7. Make notes about important details.

This includes specific notes about damage to all vehicles involved. If there were any witnesses to the crash, get their names, addresses, and phone numbers. Also note specific details about the location, weather conditions, visibility, speed limits, etc.

*document the damage*

## 8. Call your insurance company or agent.

There should be an 800 number on your insurance cards. Call as soon as possible—even while you're at the scene. That way, the details will be fresh in your mind.

## 9. Don't sign anything at the scene of the crash.

One exception: Sign whatever the police require you to sign.

## 10. Make sure you aren't injured.

Adrenalin can mask the signs of an injury, so if you have any question at all, see a doctor.

## 11. File a collision report if the police don't respond to the scene.

In some states, the police may not respond if there are no injuries, but you'll need a police report later when you file your insurance claim.

**Memorize this page and then toss the book in your glove compartment.**

# EXTREME SCENARIOS:
## WHAT TO DO WHEN THE WORST HAPPENS

Unless you've always dreamed about being Mel Gibson, Sylvester Stallone, and Ahhh-nold (no last name needed) all rolled into one, you probably can't picture yourself driving your car off a bridge and plunging into icy water 20 feet deep. But what if it happens? Would you know what to do next? Check out this extreme situation—and two other worst-case scenarios—and find out how to handle them.

## HOW TO ESCAPE FROM A SINKING CAR

1. **Unbuckle your seatbelt immediately!**
2. **Roll down the windows and unlock the doors while the electrical system is still working.**

3. **Go out an open window.**
   The car will probably float for a few seconds or minutes. This is your best chance to escape through an open window.

4. **If you can't escape while the car is still floating, go to plan B.**
   You won't be able to open the doors yet because the water pressure outside the car is too great. Wait and stay calm.

5. **Let the car begin to fill up with water.**
   When the water reaches your neck, you'll be able to open the doors. If you can't open the door, your last chance will be to break a window and crawl through it.

6. **Take a deep breath and swim to the surface.**

7. **Don't get disoriented under water.**
   The front end of the car is heavier so it will sink first. With the car nose-down, you may be confused about which way is up. Or if the water is very deep, the car may have tumbled onto its roof. Let your body float toward the surface, or follow the direction of the air bubbles as you exhale.

**Have your keys out and ready before you approach your car in a parking lot, especially at night.**

- **Keep your valuables out of sight.**
- **If a carjacker confronts you with a weapon, don't resist.**
  Give up your car willingly and get out of the way.
- **Be alert at intersections.**
  Many carjackings happen when a car is stopped at a light or stop sign.
- **Be suspicious if someone approaches your car.**
- **Be extra cautious if someone bumps your car from behind on purpose.**
  A common carjacking scenario goes like this: The carjacker bumps your car, you jump out to inspect the damage, and then the carjacker's accomplice leaps into your car and drives off. Moral of the story: If you're hit from behind in traffic and want to get out of your car to see how bad your bumper looks, take your keys with you.
- **Never get into your car at night without first checking to make sure someone isn't hiding inside.**
- **Have your keys out and ready before you approach your car in a parking lot, especially at night.**
- **If you see anyone suspicious hanging around your car as you approach it, keep walking and go find help.**

# CARJACKING: DON'T BE THE NEXT VICTIM

There are no guaranteed, foolproof ways to avoid becoming the victim of a crime, and this guide can't promise you the perfect solution for every situation. But here are some tips from the experts to keep in the back of your mind. Remember: Use your own judgment if an unexpected situation arises. It's your life on the line, and only you can judge what's likely to work best to keep you safe.

- **When pumping gas, don't leave your keys or purse in the car, and don't leave the car door standing open.**
  Take your keys and lock the car while you pump. Carjackers have been known to rush up to unoccupied cars at a gas station, jump in, and speed away.
- **Keep your car doors locked when you're driving.**

*pay attention at the gas station*

39

# ROAD RAGE

## OR, HOW I LEARNED TO STOP WORRYING AND LOVE THE DRIVER IN FRONT OF ME

You've got to be kidding me! Did you see this jerk just cut us off in the previous chapter? This has got to be some of the worst driving in the whole ruddy history of bad driving! Get off the road, buddy, before we...

Oh, hang on. Excuse us. We got carried away, which is what happens when you let your emotions get the better of you. Road rage seems to be on the upswing these days, thanks to the complete idiot jerks out there who can't stop calling names and screaming at other drivers just for simply minding their own business, when it's the other guy who's taking up too much room and ought to go back to driver's ed, you big lug-head!

Uh-oh. Lost our temper again. Our mistake. What we meant to say is that road rage is a scourge on our nation's highways and surface roads—and in some cases, a deadly scourge, which is obviously the worst kind of scourge you can have. One might go further and say that only the rankly immature, devoid of morals or self-control, would ever indulge in the kind of aggressive behavior associated with road rage.

But that doesn't stop a whole lot of people from blowing a gasket and taking out their anger on whoever or whatever is in their path.

Bottom line: Many drivers today are operating their vehicles more aggressively. And there's no doubt that drivers who drive aggressively are more likely to get involved in road rage incidents.

You don't want to get in the way of someone who's angry and happens to be behind the wheel of a massive, powerful machine, right? Of course not.

Here are some tips for dealing with road rage when it happens, and maybe even preventing it.

### Don't Make Rude Gestures:
Think of the road as a crowded, rowdy bar. If you're likely to provoke a fight in the bar, you're likely to provoke a fight on the road. The only difference is that in the bar, your opponent isn't likely to weigh several thousand pounds and be made of steel.

### Don't React to Rude Gestures:
In some cultures, extending one's middle finger means, "I'm dreadfully sorry I just veered in front of you without warning." At least it might mean that. Assume the best, and don't pick a fight.

## Stay In Your Car If You're Angry:

Did the guy behind you just beep his horn for no reason? Don't blow your cool or flip him off, and whatever you do, don't get out of your car. You never know when the guy behind you will be packing an Uzi, and in the mood to use it, too.

## Use Your Turn Signals:

Not only is telling other drivers where you're going friendly, it may actually be safer, too. Again, remember the basic premise: Try not to make the creep in the car behind you—the one who's on his way home from his anger management class—furious.

## Slower Traffic, Keep Right:

Even if you're going the speed limit (hey, even if you're going over the speed limit), you should still stay in the right lane except when passing, so that faster traffic can pass you on the left.

## Don't Tailgate:

It will not get you to your destination any faster, and will often anger the car in front of you. Also, guess who's legally at fault if you rear-end the guy in front of you. No, not him. We don't care if he was only doing 42 on the highway.

## Let Tailgaters Pass:

Pull over; slow down; do whatever you can to avoid further angering the guy behind you who's trying to shave precious seconds off his trip to the video store.

## Don't Make Eye Contact:

Studies show that angry drivers often get angrier if you make eye contact—especially insolent, provocative eye contact—with them. Keep your eyes on the road, and ignore any enraged drivers who try to get your attention.

## Leave Early:

A fairly simple concept, but one which can do wonders for your peace of mind while caught in traffic—leave early enough that nothing can make you late, then relax and let things flow.

## If You're Being Followed, Drive Straight to a Police Station:

It's impossible to guess when standard road rage will turn into something more serious. Anytime you're being followed by an enraged driver, your best bet is to drive to a police station. If you can't get to a police station, drive to a well-lit, very populated parking lot where you can safely get out, go into a store, and ask them to call the police.

*don't react!*

**Bottom line: You don't want to get in the way of someone who's angry and happens to be behind the wheel of a massive, powerful machine.**

# ALL ABOUT MAINTENANCE AND REPAIRS

## Have You Named Your Car?

Face facts. If you've named your car, you're in what can only be called a long term relationship with it. And you know how relationships go. At first everything's all fine dining, champagne, and afterglow. But after a few months, you're opening a can of soup for dinner and fighting over the remote.

Same with cars. The first few months are the honeymoon—you park your car in the far corner of the lot at the super-market, so no one will ding your new paint job, and wouldn't dream of leaving an empty coffee container on the front seat. But time goes by, and pretty soon you and "Harold" (or "Stella" or "The Demon-mobile") are like an old married couple—you're forgetting to change the oil, and haven't taken him out to the car wash in 3 weeks.

i'm taking care of this one

Can this marriage be saved?

Sure. Just turn the page and check out all the basics you need to know to keep your car running smoothly. You'll be amazed at how much longer your car will last if you just take care of a few basics, like keeping air in the tires, and keeping the oil topped off. Who knows? Treat her right, and you and Stella may even be celebrating anniversaries together for many years to come.

# THE BASICS
# A CHECKLIST

Here's a bare-bones checklist of the things
you should do regularly to keep your car
happy. For a printable copy of this chart,
go to www.realuguides.com. In the meantime,
read on to find out all the important details,
and a timetable for each task.

| CAR CARE TASK | HOW OFTEN |
| --- | --- |
| Change the oil and oil filter | every 5,000 miles or every 4 months |
| Change the air filter | every 15,000 miles or 6 months, |
| Keep your tires inflated properly | check them every 2 weeks |
| Check your headlights, parking lights, backup lights and turn signals to make sure they're all working | once a month |
| Have your brakes inspected by a professional | every 15,000 miles or 12 months, or whenever you hear a loud screeching sound when applying the brakes |
| Have a tune-up on schedule, according to your owner's manual | usually every 30,000 miles or every 12 months |
| Refill wiper/washer fluid | regularly |
| Change your windshield wiper blades | when they get so brittle that streaking occurs |
| Check the brake, power steering, transmission, and coolant fluid levels | every 3,000 miles or every 3 months |
| Rotate your tires | every 6000 miles if you're going to rotate them at all—see Page 57 for more |
| Check your battery terminals and remove any corrosion | once a year |
| Keep your car washed and waxed to protect the paint | wash every week, wax every 2 months |
| Treat weather-stripping around windows and doors with silicone spray | once a year |
| Touch up nicks and dings with touch-up paint | as needed |

# 5

# FABULOUS FLUIDS

The five fluids that matter most to your car are: oil, brake fluid, transmission fluid, coolant, power steering fluid. "What?" you're saying, "not gasoline?" Okay, sure. Without gas, you can't really go anywhere, and if you never actually drive your car, things tend to get all dry and brittle and crudded and rusty under the hood.

But without the five fabulous fluids, you aren't going anywhere, no matter how much gas you pump into your tank.

So here's the skinny on each fluid, why you need it, and how to replace it if it runs low. And if you read all the way to the end of this chapter, we'll give you the ins and outs on gasoline, too, just for being so good.

## RULE #1—
## FILTERS ARE YOUR FRIENDS

One key rule to remember about the five fabulous fluids is this: Whenever you change a fluid, change the filter that goes with it.

## 1. OIL:
## LIKE A MILKSHAKE, ONLY MESSIER

Gas makes your car go, but if you don't keep an eye on your oil, your coach might actually turn into a pumpkin at midnight—or at least something that'll take you about as far as the average pumpkin. Oil keeps your engine running, and without it, or without the right amounts at the right times, your car can become little more than a couple tons of ugly, useless, immobile steel.

Here's everything you need to know about paying homage to the king of grease.

### Why Should You Change Your Oil?

Oil performs a lot of different functions in your car—things like keeping it clean and lubricated, cushioning moving parts, and cooling the engine. But one if its most important functions is trapping the sludge and chemical bi-products of the engine and keeping them from contaminating the moving parts. Oil can only hold so much sludge, though, before it becomes thick and soupy and grumpy and ceases to perform its other important functions. That's why you need to change it periodically, and may also need to "top it off" by adding a quart between oil changes.

### When Should You Change Your Oil?

Here's another case in which the owner's manual should be your guide. The standard recommendation is to change your oil every 5,000 miles, but if your manual recommends something different, take their word for it, not ours. In fact, if you don't change your oil when your manual tells you to, you can even void your warranty—which is bad news if you run into real problems that are often the result of, say, not having changed your oil often enough.

### Service Ratings

Whether you're topping off the oil in your car or getting a complete oil change, the most important thing to look for in your new oil is the American Petroleum Institute (API) service rating. You can find out what API service rating your car needs by checking the owner's manual. As of 2004, the latest service ratings are "SJ" and "SL." You can always use oil that has a newer service rating than your car requires, but you can't use oil with an older service rating, such as "SA" through "SH," except in much older cars. Diesel engines will also require a special API service rating, starting with the letter "C."

### Pick a Viscosity, Any Viscosity

Motor oils, like milkshakes, come in different "viscosities," or thicknesses. The most commonly recommended viscosities are 5W-30 and 10W-30, and these are fine for pretty much any newer car. The first number (5W or 10W) indicates the temperature range at which the oil flows best. 5W-30 flows better in the winter, and 10W-30 flows better in the summer. But this difference is slight, and there's little need to change your viscosity to match the season. More important, again, is your owner's manual recommendation. For example, cars with turbo charged engines will often require 10W-40 because it can withstand hotter engine temperatures.

### Synthetic Oils vs. Natural Oils

You know that all-polyester shirt you own which never needs to be washed, or dried, or ironed, just needs to be shaken out from time to time? Synthetic oil works kind of like that: It lasts much longer in your engine, and can withstand more extreme temperatures and conditions.

However, synthetic oil has another similarity to your synthetic, shiny wardrobe: You're not likely to run into those extreme conditions in which it's really appropriate unless you're driving in the desert or the tundra (or in the case of the shirt, attending a lot of Euro-pop dance parties).

And since synthetic oils don't need to be changed as often as natural oils, you may run into the problem of voiding your warranty by not changing your oil often enough. Of course, you could change your synthetic oil every 5,000 miles, but that would be expensive, and it kind of defeats the purpose of buying synthetic in the first place. Best to stick with the natural look unless your owner's manual specifies synthetic oil.

# HOW TO CHECK FLUID LEVELS

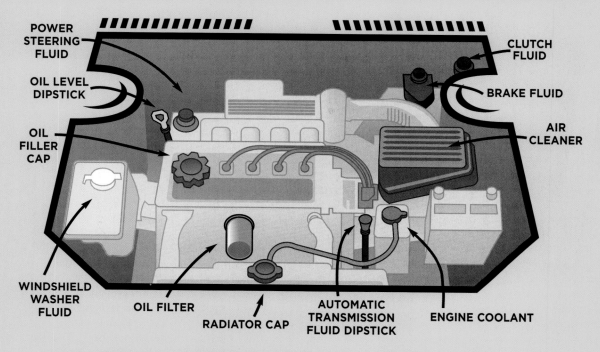

**POWER STEERING FLUID**

**OIL LEVEL DIPSTICK**

**OIL FILLER CAP**

**WINDSHIELD WASHER FLUID**

**OIL FILTER**

**RADIATOR CAP**

**AUTOMATIC TRANSMISSION FLUID DIPSTICK**

**ENGINE COOLANT**

**CLUTCH FLUID**

**BRAKE FLUID**

**AIR CLEANER**

Here's a look at a typical engine, to give you an idea about where you might find various fluid containers. Each car is different, though, so check your owner's manual to find out where these things are located under your car's hood.

## 2. COOLANT

Coolant and anti-freeze are two names for the same thing, which is completely baffling since they sound like they should perform opposite functions. Basically, coolant goes in your radiator and keeps the car's engine cool in warm weather. Anti-freeze—the exact same stuff— keeps the engine warm in the winter. On modern cars, coolant is added to the plastic tank that feeds into the radiator, not to the radiator itself. You'll want to flush it out and replace it with new coolant every 2 years in warm climates, every year in cold climates. Check your manual for more details.

## 3. BRAKE FLUID

Under normal circumstances, you shouldn't need to replace your brake fluid because it doesn't evaporate. But if you've got a leak, the fluid's going to obey the laws of gravity and find its way to the ground. This could be a major safety issue since the brake fluid is an essential component of the braking system and you want your brakes to work 100% of the time—not just most of the time. So check the container every 3 months and top off if the level has dropped to more than half an inch below the top of the container. Make sure you add brand new fluid from an unopened container—you don't want to use old, possibly

*should've changed the oil*

## 5. TRANSMISSION FLUID

The nice thing about transmission fluid is that it comes in colors, usually pink or green. (Sometimes it's clear.) You can test your transmission fluid by putting a drop of it on a clean white cloth or paper towel.

If it's still pink, green, or clear, it's probably still fine. If it's creamy like strawberry yogurt, you may have a leak which will need to be repaired. If it's dirty, burnt-smelling, and dark red or brown, it's time to replace it. In general, you don't need to change this fluid very often. Some manufacturers say every 30,000 miles. Some experts say even that often is overkill. Best plan: Do what your owner's manual tells you to do. Better safe than sorry when it comes to something as major as a transmission. (Unless you actually like the idea of driving around in only one gear!)

contaminated brake fluid, which can just gum up the works. Consult your owner's manual for the type of fluid to use, and for more details.

## 4. POWER STEERING FLUID

Without this stuff, your car will begin to make hideous noises, and you won't be able to turn the wheel easily. Most people find this an undesirable circumstance. If you share that majority view, check the power steering fluid every 3 months, and top off as needed. You should keep the reservoir filled to somewhere above the "add" line and below the "full" line. Buy power steering fluid by the quart at most auto supply stores. Have it completely replaced every 2 years.

*steering stiff? check the power steering fluid*

# FILL 'ER UP, MACK: ALL ABOUT GAS

You can think of gasoline as the "fluid" that keeps your "car" "running"—hey, for all we care, you can think of it as the "magic fairy dust" that makes your "witches broom fly through the air." Either way, you don't have much choice about whether to buy it.

The choice you do have is which octane to buy. Here's the good news about gas octane: There's absolutely no reason to buy anything more than the minimum recommended by your owner's manual.

Of course, by labeling premium octane gas with names like "Super-Fabulous" or "Fantastico!" or even just, say, calling it "Premium," gas companies are trying to get you to believe that higher octane gas is better for your car, worth the extra money, and might even give you x-ray vision. Not so on any count. Your car is designed to run best with the octane recommended by your owner's manual. It's true that some cars—those with high compression engines—need higher octane gasoline. But for everyone else, regular is not only fine, it's the best way to go.

# ✚ CHARGE! TAKING CARE OF BATTERIES ⊖

Most modern batteries are "maintenance free," which means that you don't usually have to do anything to them. But some batteries require maintenance—you've got to add water on a regular basis.

1. **If you have a non-maintenance-free battery, remove the caps from the top of your battery and check in each well to see if the water covers the metal plates inside.**

2. **If you can see the metal plates sticking up above the water level, add some distilled water.**

   Pour in just enough to cover the plates. Always use distilled water (never tap water), which is available at the grocery store.

3. **While you're at it, you'll want to check the battery terminals for corrosion.**

   Do this with the engine OFF! And be very careful: Wear gloves and goggles, and never touch both terminals at the same time with your hands or any tools.

4. **Remove the battery cables from the terminal.**

   If you can't get them off easily, you may need to buy a tool called a battery terminal puller. Or get a pro to do this.

5. **Use a metal brush to remove any corrosion.**

6. **Coat each battery post or terminal with petroleum jelly.**

7. **Reattach the cables and tighten them securely, but not so tight that you crack the battery case.**

**49**

### Oil Light (Red):
Indicates that the oil has gotten low. You must react to this immediately by adding oil, or you can ruin your engine.

### Battery Light (Red):
Indicates that the battery is not charging properly or may need to be replaced. Turn off all electric accessories in your car (radio, A/C, etc.) and drive directly to a service station. If you ignore this light, your car may stop running, and probably won't start again until you've charged the battery.

### Brake Light (Red):
Generally indicates that the parking brake is on. If it comes on when you're driving, pull over and make sure the parking brake is off. If the brake light stays on, you may have a serious problem with the brakes. Tow the car to a mechanic.

### Coolant Light (Red):
Although not found on all cars, this indicates that your coolant level is low. Stop driving and top off the coolant. If it comes on again, you may have a coolant leak. See a mechanic.

Although the dashboard indicator lights on every car are slightly different, most follow a fairly intuitive color-coding system. Red lights require immediate attention—usually along the lines of turning off your car and calling for a tow truck in many cases. Amber or yellow lights are warnings that something is not right with your system, and you should have it checked soon. And green lights are just there for your entertainment—or it means you've got your turn signal on.

Here's a quick list of common dashboard lights and what they usually mean, although if one of them comes on, it's always a good idea to double check your manual and see what the manufacturer has to say about it.

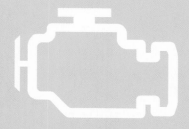

### Check Engine Light (Amber or Yellow):

Indicates that something is wrong with the fuel system or the fuel injection system. It may be as simple as a loose gas cap, or something more serious. If it comes on more than once, and cannot be fixed by tightening the gas cap, go to a mechanic.

### ABS Light (Amber or Yellow):

Indicates that there may be a problem with the Antilock Braking System. Although you will still be able to brake normally, the antilock brakes may not work if this light is on.

### SRS Light (Amber or Yellow):

Indicates that there is something wrong with your airbag system. (SRS stands for Supplemental Restraint System.) Have it checked out immediately— and drive carefully on the way.

### Fuel Light (Amber or Yellow):

Gas is low. You can check your manual to find out approximately how much gas is left in the tank when this light comes on, but you'd be better off just driving immediately to a gas station and filling up.

# RUBBER,
# MEET THE ROAD

**Your tires are your first line of defense against a lot of unfortunate scenarios, including the really undesirable scenario in which your car is careening down the road at 60 mph on its chassis. Okay, admittedly that's not going to happen unless you have 4 simultaneous blowouts, which isn't too likely. Still, why take the chance?**

**There are 4 basic rules for keeping your tires in good shape:**

**1** keep them properly inflated and be sure to use
a quality tire gauge to check them before you drive

**2** rotate them regularly

**3** keep them aligned and balanced

**4** replace them when the tread is gone

# TIRE INFLATION BASICS

Keeping your tires properly inflated is one of the easiest, simplest, and cheapest ways to avoid a number of disasters. After all, air is free—even that spiffy compressed air they cram into those machines at the gas station. Use it properly, and you'll avoid a whole passel of problems. Read on!

**1. Find the proper tire pressure for your tires.**

It's listed in your owner's manual and also on the door jamb, usually on the driver's side, sometimes on the passenger side, just to keep you on your toes. The front and rear tires may take slightly different amounts of pressure, indicated, cleverly enough, by the letters "F" and "R." The number will be listed in PSI, which stands for "pounds per square inch."

**2. Buy a tire gauge.**

It should look like a pen with an extendible "tongue." If it does not—if it looks, for example, like a swordfish wearing sock garters—you have purchased the wrong thing. Try again.

**3. Check the pressure.**

If there is not enough, add air until there is. Don't use the tire gauge that is attached to the air hose at your service station—we've heard it's fishy at best. Use your own pen-shaped one.

**4. When using the tire gauge, insert it firmly into the valve.**

Otherwise, you may not get an accurate reading. Also, always check your tires when they're "cold" (which means that they haven't been driven more than a mile).

**5. Ignore the tire pressure listed on the sidewalls of your tires.**

That's usually the maximum pressure the tire can withstand—not the recommended pressure. Of course you should never inflate the tire beyond the maximum pressure allowed.

**6. Be especially alert when the seasons change.**

Cold air outdoors will affect your tire pressure, causing it to drop.

**7. If for some reason you've got too much air in your tire, let air out by pressing something—your pen-shaped tire gauge, for example—into the valve.**

You should hear a hissing sound. If you instead hear Celine Dion, turn down your radio and try again.

**8. Remember that over time, the air leaks out of your tires, so you'll have to refill them.**

Check them once a week, or more often if you really enjoy watching the plastic tongue shoot out of your pen-shaped gauge and it's become your primary form of entertainment.

blowout!

# IT'S NOT HOT AIR...

**Here's a quick list of five ugly consequences you'll face if you don't keep your tires properly inflated.**

## 1. Blowouts

Under- or overinflated tires can cause blowouts which can lead to crashes, the need to change your own tire or, worst case, standing by the side of the road in heels for an hour waiting for a tow-truck—even more embarrassing if you're a guy.

## 2. Uneven Tire Wear

If your tires are consistently inflated improperly, you'll know it just by looking at the tread. And guess what? They'll wear out faster. Do you really want to buy new tires every year instead of buying that spiffy new stereo system for the bedroom? See the sidebar at right for a key to How to Read the Tread. (Note: Improper tire inflation isn't the only explanation for uneven tire wear. If your car's been in a collision and the body no longer even remotely resembles a rectangle, you may also see signs of uneven tire wear. Ditto if your wheels aren't balanced and/or aligned.)

## 3. Bad Handling

A car with improper tire pressure won't steer as well as it should.

## 4. Rough Ride

Over-inflated tires produce a bumpier, bouncier ride.

## 5. Bad Fuel Economy

If your tires are under-inflated, you'll get fewer miles to the gallon.

**If your tires are under-inflated, you'll get fewer miles to the gallon.**

# HOW TO READ THE TREAD

**NORMAL**

**OVERINFLATED**

**Worn in the middle:**
If the middle of your tire's going bald but it's still got a full head of, um, tread on the sides, it's overinflated.

**UNDERINFLATED**

**Worn on both sides:**
If it's starting to get that "faux-hawk" look—tread in the middle, bald on the sides—it's either consistently underinflated, or you may need a wheel alignment.

**SCALLOPS**

**Worn in cup shapes or scallops:**
This is the classic sign of a bent suspension, but it can also mean that your wheels need to be balanced.

**OUT OF ALIGNMENT**

**Worn on one side only:**
This usually means that you've got an alignment problem.

**BALD SPOTS**

**Worn in patches:**
Irregular wear can mean a defective tire or, more likely, your wheel needs to be balanced.

# CHECK THE AIR IN YOUR SPARE

Good news: You got a flat tire, but you masterfully managed to change to your spare tire all by yourself, with minimal cursing or embarrassment. Too bad you've never checked the air in your spare, and it's as flat as the one you just took off. Get the idea?

## BALANCING YOUR TIRES

Despite such modern manufacturing miracles as the mini CD, the doughnut hole, and the lighted spinning yo-yo, the tires on your car are not perfectly round. You'd see just how imperfect they are if you jacked your car up and then watched one of the tires spin, mounted on the wheel, producing a noticeable wobble.

Luckily there's a perfectly adequate way to deal with this problem. Auto experts can (and should) balance your tires every time they mount them on the rims, by adding small weights to the wheels to make them spin properly.

Once they're balanced, however, your wheels should stay that way, and you won't have to rebalance them—even when you rotate your tires—unless the little weights fall off in a crash. (In that case, though, you may have to rebalance a lot of things, including your checkbook.)

## TIRES, GET IN LINE

Alignment is a fairly complex procedure which is done to make sure your wheels point in the right direction. Here's what you need to know and why it matters:

• If you ever take your hands off the steering wheel while you're driving (and we don't recommend that), and the car pulls to the left or right, your wheels may be out of alignment.

• Most cars need routine realignment every six months, and sometimes more frequently if you've hit a large hole or a curb, causing your wheels to be misaligned.

• If your car's front end vibrates at high speeds, the wheels may be out of balance or out of alignment. Try balancing the wheels first—it's cheaper.

If your car pulls to the left or right, or if your car's front end vibrates at high speeds, your wheels may be out of alignment.

# THE TRUTH ABOUT TIRE ROTATION

Car gurus say you should rotate your tires every 6,000 miles in order to preserve and extend the life of the tread. This is basically accurate advice. With radial tires, you usually swap them from front to back and vice versa—keeping the left tires on the left side, and the right on the right—and it can help even out the wear patterns in the tread.

Fine. There's only one problem. Occasionally you'll find that right after you've rotated your tires, suddenly there's a vibration in the steering column that's vaguely reminiscent of the Magic Fingers at a cheap motel. This can happen if one of the back wheels was damaged or bent—usually the result of driving over a pothole. Now that it's on the front of the car, you really notice it because the bent wheel's irregular motion is being transmitted to the steering column.

The fix is simply to put the tires back where they were—and soon, before the new position results in a blowout. Bottom line: Rotate your tires unless when you do, you hate the results.

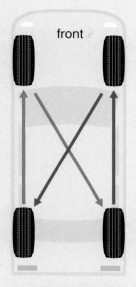

**REAR WHEEL DRIVE**

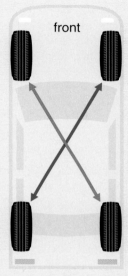

**FOUR WHEEL DRIVE**

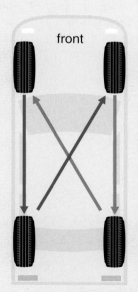

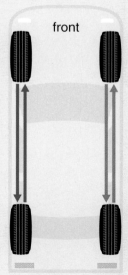

**FRONT WHEEL DRIVE (EITHER)**

# WHEN TO BUY NEW TIRES

If you keep your wheels aligned, rotate your tires, and keep the tires properly inflated, your tires should have a good long life. How long? That depends on how you drive your car, and where, and in what kind of weather. Tire life varies based on a lot of conditions. Some tires will last 40,000 miles, just as the manufacturer predicts. Others are gone long before they hit that mark.

But you should definitely consider buying new tires when the tread is down to 1/16 of an inch. Why? Because the tread is a key safety feature. It helps the car grip the road during braking and cornering, and also prevents hydroplaning, which is what happens when the car literally floats on the water covering the road surface during a storm.

Most new tires have tread wear indicators that appear as bars across the width of the tire when the tire wears out. You should definitely replace your tires when those bars appear, and maybe even sooner.

But the actual purchase of new tires can be tricky. You're often buying them because one of your tires is leaking, flat, or both, and you need the new set right away. (Notice how we said "new set?" If you're buying one new tire, you should be buying two. Always replace your tires in pairs.) So you're often willing to take whatever the nearest auto supply shop has to offer.

So how do you know you're getting the right thing? Check your owner's manual and ask for tires that are the same size as the originals. And check out the chart on the opposite page for more info.

## Checking Your Tread:
## The Only Remaining Good Use for a Penny

To find out if you have enough tread left on your tires, insert a penny into one of the grooves in the tread. Put the penny in with Abe Lincoln's head facing down, toward the tire—not up toward the sky. If the tread is still deep enough, you won't be able to see the top of Lincoln's head. If you can see the top of his head, buy new tires.

# HOW TO READ YOUR SIDEWALLS

There's a wealth of information about your tires molded into the rubber of your sidewalls. Here's what some of it means.

**SPEED RATING SYMBOLS**

| Rating | Max Speed in MPH |
|--------|------------------|
| S | 112 |
| T | 118 |
| U | 124 |
| H | 130 |
| V | 149 |
| Z | Over 149 |

Ratio of Height to Width (aspect ratio)

Width of Tire (in millimeters)

"R" stands for Radial

Diameter of Wheel (in inches)

"P" stands for Passenger Car Tire

Tire Ply Composition and Materials Used

Load Index and Speed Symbol

**P205/65R15 91T**

ROADHOG XYZ

TREAD 2PLY STEEL + 2PLY POLYESTER SIDEWALL 2PLY POLYESTER

TUBELESS MAX LOAD 1400 LBS. AT 35 PSI MAX PRESS STANDARD LOAD

TIRE MFG.

TREADWEAR 300 TRACTION B TEMPERATURE B

DOT UR U9

Max Cold Inflation Load Limit

Tire Name

US Dot Safety Standard Code

Temperature: Rated A through C. A is highest.

Traction: Rated AA, A, B, or C. AA is the highest.

Treadwear: This tire, rated 300, will last 3 times as long as a tire rated 100.

# NAME THAT TUNE-UP

Cars, like aging pop stars' careers, occasionally need some professional service in order to keep churning out forgettable gold records... or, er, to keep driving, as the case may be. However, not all tune-ups are created equal.

Some can be as simple as an oil and filter change (the pop star equivalent of a new wardrobe and an HBO concert special), while others can be as extensive as a complete check-up and overhaul of all the systems that make your engine run (the pop star equivalent of a new nose, a new label, and an embarrassingly desperate "Duets" album featuring younger, more popular stars). Here are some basic tips for when it's time to revamp your career.

## TUNE-UPS TIPS:

■ The basic 10,000 mile tune-up, which included new spark plugs, timing belt adjustment, and filter changes, is basically a thing of the past. Cars built in the 1980's or later have computers that take care of these basics, and the Check Engine Light automatically comes on if there's a problem.

■ The schedule for newer cars looks more like this: oil and oil filter change every 5,000 miles, and more major service every 30,000 miles. Your manual will have a more specific schedule. Take their word for it if their recommendations are different from ours (although most experts insist that the 5,000 mile oil change is the standard, even if the manufacturer recommends a longer term).

■ The services which are required every 30,000 miles include an oil and filter change, but they'll also include a laundry list of engine parts which must be checked and replaced if they're not in good shape—parts like the air filter, belts, spark plugs, hoses, etc. The shop should also check your wheel alignment, rotate your tires, etc. A list of what should be done at each 30,000-mile service can be found somewhere in your owner's manual. If you take your car into a dealership for service, they'll have this list on hand.

# WHENS AND WHYS OF MAJOR SERVICE

*100,000 miles & still running!*

### WHEN:
**Major service will only be necessary every 30,000 miles or 12 months.**

Some manuals may recommend major service before you hit 30,000 miles, but experts say this isn't necessary, unless failing to get the service will void your warranty.

### WHY:
**There are three main reasons to keep up with major service.**

The first is to make sure all parts are operating normally so that a breakdown on the road does not occur. Major service will check any number of the things that tend to go wrong with older cars, or cars with a lot of miles on them. Better to catch something like a worn belt now, rather than in the middle of your road trip to Mexico.

The second reason is to preserve and extend the life of your car. You want to be driving "Stella" for many years to come, right?

And the third is your warranty—many warranties will be voided if you don't bring in the car for "regularly scheduled maintenance," i.e., major service.

**"But I Hardly Ever Drive It!"**
If you don't drive your car very often, you'll have to take it in for an oil change—and major service—*before* you hit the mileage requirements. Why? Because belts can dry out and fluids can go bad over time even if you're not driving the car. Your manual should list a maintenance schedule based on time as well as mileage. Check it and obey.

> Better to catch something like a worn belt now, rather than in the middle of your road trip to Mexico.

61

# DEALERSHIP VS. INDEPENDENT MECHANIC TUNE-UPS

There is no shortage of places you can take your car when it's time to get it serviced, and each offers different advantages.

Here's a run-down of some pros and cons for dealership service, independent mechanic service, and "Quickie" service shops. Remember that no matter what type of shop you take your car to, you should make sure you trust the mechanic first. If you're looking for independent mechanics, auto repair facilities with ASE (Automotive Service Excellence) certified mechanics and those that participate in AAA's Approved Auto Repair Network are an excellent place to start. Also, ask friends for recommendations and check out your Better Business Bureau for any complaints BEFORE you use the repair shop.

## DEALERSHIP TUNE-UPS:

- Dealership mechanics get specific training about how to service their cars, especially new model cars. Although good independent mechanics will try to keep up with new information and service procedures, the dealer will probably learn the latest procedures before the independent mechanic gets a chance.

- Dealerships have access to "silent recall" information—information about parts which are faulty and which should be replaced, but for which there has been no public recall.

- Along the same lines, dealerships receive "technical service bulletins" from the manufacturer, which can include information about new service procedures not included in the manual.

- If a dealership finds a problem with a part which is covered under your warranty, they'll fix it without charging you.

- Dealerships also have better access to specific parts needed for your car—after all, they represent the manufacturer directly.

- Dealerships tend to charge more for service—sometimes a lot more. And for a basic service like an oil and filter change, the dealership isn't going to do anything that your trusted independent mechanic can't do.

- You don't have to take a car into the dealership in order to maintain your warranty. By law, the dealership must honor your warranty whether you've had regular maintenance performed by the dealership or by an independent mechanic. Just be sure to keep all records of any repairs made, including every oil change.

## INDEPENDENT MECHANIC TUNE-UPS:

- For basic service, independent mechanics are generally much cheaper than the dealership would be. In fact, for every kind of service, independent mechanics tend to be cheaper than dealerships.

- If you have a relationship with an independent mechanic whom you trust, it may be smart to keep that relationship going, in case you run into big trouble later and have to get down on your knees and beg for reasonably-priced assistance.

- The corner mechanic won't automatically have access to the latest technical service bulletins and recall information, but if you're savvy, you might be able to get this information yourself from the manufacturer's website, or another car maintenance website, and bring it to your mechanic.

- Independent mechanics may not have easy access to parts for your car, nor to the specific dealer-recommended fluids.

## QUICKIE OIL CHANGE SHOPS:

Although probably fine for a simple oil and filter change, most experts recommend against using these shops for anything even slightly more complicated than changing your oil. And even for an oil change, watch them as they work. Some quickie shops have been known to cut corners —including the corner called "actually changing the oil."

Be particularly wary if one of these quickie shops claims to be able to do a major tune-up for a low price. That kind of service is best left to a full-fledged mechanic.

Anytime you take your car to a quickie shop, request brand-name fluids and filters, and watch the mechanics performing the service. If you're not happy, feel free to speak up.

## BEYOND TUNE-UPS: HOW TO LOVE YOUR CAR

Sure, it's important to maintain the stuff under the hood. But don't forget to give your car's exterior its regular maintenance, too— in the form of a weekly wash job, and a wax job every two months or whenever water stops beading on the surface. Keeping the paint looking good is the best way to make sure that when it's time to sell, you'll get top dollar—and can go out and buy another car you'll love just as much.

# MORE REAL U...

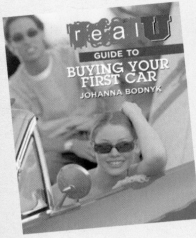

## BUYING YOUR FIRST CAR

Don't get burned on the first big purchase you make. Find out how to get the best financing, how to avoid the latest scam tactics, whether to buy extended warranties, and more.

## TRAVELING ON YOUR OWN

Whether you're making your first trips to visit out-of-state colleges, hitting the road for Spring Break, or just visiting relatives, this guide is your ticket to an excellent adventure. By Peter Greenberg, travel editor of NBC's *Today Show* and the author of *The Travel Detective*.

## CHECK OUT THESE OTHER REAL U GUIDES!

Your First Apartment

Living on Your Own

Planning for College

Bank Accounts and Credit Cards

Saving and Investing

Your First Job

Identity Theft

## FOR MORE INFORMATION, VISIT WWW.REALUGUIDES.COM